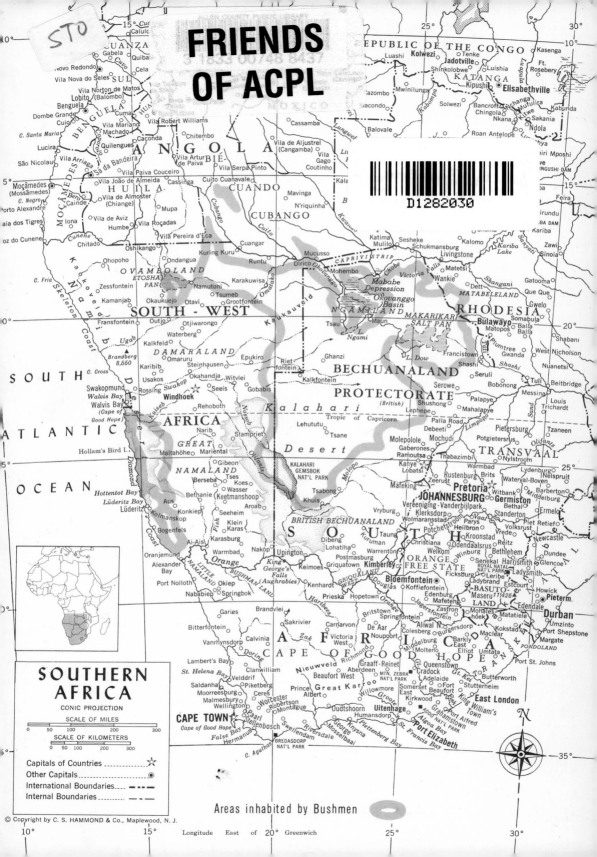

FRIENDS OF ACPL

D1282030

SOUTHERN AFRICA

CONIC PROJECTION

SCALE OF MILES

0   50   100   200   300

SCALE OF KILOMETERS

0   50   100   200   300

Capitals of Countries .... ☆
Other Capitals .... ◉
International Boundaries.... ▬ ▬ ▬
Internal Boundaries .... ▬ · ▬ · ▬

Areas inhabited by Bushmen

Longitude   East   of   20°   Greenwich

"I Saw You from Afar"

"I Saw You from Afar"

A visit to the Bushmen of the
Kalahari Desert

Carol Morse Perkins
and
Marlin Perkins

ATHENEUM 1965 NEW YORK

To Alice, Fred, and Marguerite

"I Saw You from Afar"

I

We had come halfway across the world
to reach the beautiful red desert we were crossing. It is
an area of rolling sand dunes, strong yellow grass, and
patches of dense scrub, about three times the size of
England. We were there because in this famed Kalahari
Desert of South Africa live a gentle people called Bushmen, and we wanted to visit them.

The Bushmen are the oldest inhabitants of South
Africa. Once they lived in the green and fertile lands
farther south, where they had plenty of water and
game. They led happy lives, hunting and painting beautiful pictures of animals and of themselves on great
rocks and cliffs and in deep caves. Some of these paint-
ings still exist, and one may go to see them, where the
Bushmen used to live, and read the stories of their past

as told in the pictures. It has been many, many years since the Bushmen lived so well.

About the time the Pilgrims landed at Plymouth Rock, stronger tribes of men began to move down from more northern parts of Africa and white men came from Europe to the southern tip of the continent. They came to make homes and to farm the land. As the people from the north moved down and the people to the south moved up, the Bushmen were squeezed out. More and more these ancient men had to retreat to the desert, which no one else wanted, where they would be safe.

Many people believe that the Bushmen are a separate race from any other in the world. Little is really known about them. Few people have ever been able to know them. They roam in an inaccessible part of the world and speak an extremely difficult language.

They have golden skin, oriental eyes, slender hands and feet, and tightly curled black hair. Their voices are soft; and they speak a click language, full of sharp pops and clicks made with the tongue in the back of the mouth.

Most Bushmen are less than five feet tall. They are sensitive about their small size, and so they often greet each other by saying, "I saw you from afar." This is a great compliment, implying that the one being greeted is very large indeed and can be seen from far away.

Bushmen are primarily hunters. They kill their game with bows and poisoned arrows. In addition to meat, they eat roots that they dig from the ground and the melons and berries that grow in the desert. Living in small family communities, they move about the desert carrying their few skins and bows and arrows with them. They stop wherever they can find food; and when it is gone, they move on. Although the area where they live has changed, their actual way of life may not have changed for 25,000 years.

Since the Bushmen have come to the desert, they have learned to eat almost anything that can be eaten, in order to survive. It is not an easy life for them, but they have filled their days with dances and stories, humor, kindness, and dignity. They laugh a great deal, and are gentle and considerate with each other.

The main problem of the Bushman in the desert is finding water. During the months of November, December, and January the rains come. The dry river beds fill with water, and for a little while the people and the animals have enough to drink. But this time is soon gone. The rivers dry up under the scorching sun and become mud flats. The land is once again a desert. Then everyone must hunt a long time to find water.

The people get some moisture from the melons they eat and from grasses that have juices in them. The main sources of actual water are places, known only to Bush-

5

men, where there is water deep beneath the sand. They dig down and suck out this water through long hollow straws. When their mouths are full, they spit the water into empty ostrich egg shells. As each shell becomes full, the hole in it is stopped up with a tuft of dry grass. Some of these shells are buried in the sand for future use, and the rest are carried in leather pouches. The knowledge of where "sip wells" are located is a carefully guarded secret, passed from father to son.

Bushmen have few treats and few delicacies to eat. The few they have, they relish. Bushmen love honey. They not only love to eat it, but they believe that eating it is a way to wisdom. It is the only sweet food the Bushmen have. They are always on the watch for bees. By following one bee home to its hive, a whole store of honey may be found. Once found, a hive is guarded as carefully by a Bushman as is his water hole. When he collects the honey, he never takes all of it; there is always some left for the bees. The hive is not seriously disturbed, and so the bees do not fly away.

Termites are another delicacy much loved by the Bushmen. A kind of flying ant, termites live in great mounds of sand, four or five feet high, shaped like conical towers. These are full of rooms and tunnels for the termites' many activities. There is one room where just the king and queen live; she never goes out as long as she is able to lay eggs.

Just before the rainy season, some of the termites develop wings a few days after they are born. These flying termites gather together and leave the mound to start a new community somewhere else. The Bushmen know many things about the world they live in; and so they know when the termites are about to leave and are prepared for them. They light a fire near a mound, which seems to draw the termites from their dark tunnels out into the light. The insects fly right into the fire and are nicely toasted. To the Bushman, this is a delicious treat. They eat all they can hold right on the spot. The rest of the termites are carried home in leather pouches to be made into soup.

There are three main groups of Bushmen still living in the Kalahari Desert. Two groups, the Heikum Bushmen who live in the eastern part and the Auen Bushmen who live in the southern part of the desert, are very few in number. The largest group is the Kung Bushmen, who live in the northwest and central Kalahari.

In 1955 it was reported that there were about 20,000 Bushmen still living in Southeast Africa. There are about 30,000 Bushmen living in the Bechuanaland Protectorate, and a few thousand are reported to be in Angola. Altogether, all the Bushmen in the world do not equal more than the total population of a town about the size of Pittsfield, Massachusetts.

These things, and some others, we knew about the Bushmen, because we had read accounts of other people's visits to them. But we wanted to see for ourselves, because we felt that they were a people we wanted very much to know. The Bushmen we hoped to find, and did find, were Auen Bushmen.

II

In a Land-Rover, an English version of the American Jeep,—which will go anywhere, up hills and down gullies, over underbrush and through tangled growth—we had come to the part of the desert where we hoped to meet some Bushmen. The farther we had come, the more anxious we were to find the people we were seeking.

We were delighted then, when one hot November afternoon, we finally saw a small figure in the distance.

We knew that we had come at last to a Bushman camp, and we hoped that they would welcome us. The Bushmen have often been taken as slaves by the men who conquered their land. So it is understandable that they are shy of strangers.

When we came nearer, we saw that our first Bushman was a boy. He was not afraid and came to greet us. Our interpreter, who spoke their click language, told the boy that we had come across the great water to visit his people and we hoped that he would take us to his family. He smiled at us and invited us to come with him to the top of the great sand dune where he had been playing. He said that his name was Nuse.

10

We climbed to the top of the dune, and there on the other side we saw the family camp. If we had not been guided to it, we might not have seen it. The grass houses of the Bushmen are so well disguised that it is possible to stand right beside one and not know it from a bush. The Bushmen call their grass shelters *Scherms*.

Sometimes a Bushman is content with a home that is merely a branch stuck into the sand, on which he hangs his few possessions, and a place for his fire. It is enough just to hollow out a place in the warm sand for a bed to lie in, out of the night air. When it is cold, children sleep beside the very old people to help them keep warm in the night. When the sun goes down in the desert, it gets quite cool, and the Bushmen have few clothes and few covers.

We walked down the soft red sand of the dune, hot from the sun, to the grassy land below. Our dream had come true. We were in the Kalahari Desert with a smiling Bushman boy, on our way to meet the people we had come halfway around the world to find.

Nuse's grandfather, called Aharob, saw us and came at once to speak to us. We presented him with a gift of tobacco, which Bushmen love, and explained our visit to their community. We hoped to camp nearby to make their acquaintance and to photograph their daily life. Aharob thanked us for our gift and invited us to come with him to meet the other members of his family.

As we were introduced, the Bushmen looked at us carefully and with great curiosity, but not rudely. They are a courteous people among themselves, and their natural good manners extend to strangers. The oldest man in the group, called Makai, met us by repeating an ancient Bushman greeting: "I was dead, but now that you have come I am alive again."

We met Gokus, the grandmother. She had black circles painted on her cheeks for decoration and was wear-
ing a necklace and earrings made of broken bits of ostrich egg shell. The pieces are polished and shaped by
rubbing them on rocks. Bushmen spend many hours
making jewelry like this, dying the pieces of egg shell
with juices of berries and stringing them on leather
thongs.

14

There were many children, lovely golden children,
smiling up at us from the warm red sand.

One little boy, Nxou, was very shy. He watched us for a long time from behind a bush before he smiled at us and came out to be our friend. We learned that he was Nuse's cousin, and was about the same age.

Since the Bushmen had welcomed us so warmly, we set up our camp nearby. In the days we stayed there, we spent as much time as we could with our new friends because they were pleasant to be with, and because all of the things they did were interesting to us.

16

III

The lives of the Bushmen are quite simple compared to our lives. They do not own many things. They do not have to know and understand many of the things people in our country are expected to know and understand. Most of their time is spent getting food and doing the things they need to do in order to survive. This does not mean that life is easy for Bushman children. They have much to learn to help them be successful in their way of life, and there are many things that they are expected to do to help the others in the camp.

On a typical morning in the Bushman camp, Nxou and his cousin, Nuse, woke very early, when it was just getting light. Nxou's name means "bowl of food". Nuse's name means "ostrich egg". When he was born, he didn't have any hair, and his parents thought that his head looked like an egg.

This morning, as on many mornings, the boys were

cold and stiff from lying on the ground. The fire had burned very low during the night, and almost all of the wood was gone. They knew what they should do. After stretching and yawning a little to be sure they were awake, they rose and ran out into the desert. It felt good to run, and soon they were warmer. Nxou found a twisted old tree that had some dry branches, and they climbed up to break them off.

The boys enjoyed the desert early in the morning

when the air was cool and sweet. The birds sang and chirped about them, and at their feet little desert mice scurried down their holes. If the boys were lucky, they might catch a turtle. There is always something to watch for and to hope for in the desert.

In a little while, Nxou's mother came to help them carry bundles of wood back to camp. His little sister came along to look for lizards. Lizards make delicious soup.

Everyone was awake now. While the boys had been gathering wood for the fire, Gausje, Nuse's sister, had been digging under bushes looking for tender roots to eat. Whatever food a Bushman finds, he shares with all the camp.

The men soon made a fire out of the wood that Nxou and Nuse had found in the desert. The Bushmen have no matches, but they have two special sticks that work just as well for them.

The sticks are about a foot long. They are thin sticks, and one of them has a small hole in the end. The stick with the hole is laid on a small pile of dry grass, with the hole over the grass. The Bushman takes the other stick and puts the tip of it into the hole, which has been carved to just the right size. Then he spins the stick around in the hole between the palms of his two hands. He spins it very fast, and in a few seconds there is a little smoke, then a spark, and then the dry grass bursts into flame. A few dry twigs are added, and then bigger ones, and soon there is a fire for cooking breakfast.

Nxou and his sister stood near the fire to warm their hands. It was still early in the morning, and the sun had not yet risen high enough in the sky to give very much heat. In a few hours it would be very hot—but not yet.

Great-grandfather Makai was also sitting by the fire to warm his old bones after the chilly night. While they were waiting for the breakfast soup to cook, the children asked him to tell them again about how the Bushmen first got fire. Makai told wonderful stories. He had told this story many times, but the children never tired of hearing it. Some day they will tell it to their children, and their children will tell it in turn to their children. In this way the legends of the Bushman, and the learnings he has acquired, have come down through the ages and will be passed on.

IV

The children already knew about Mantis. The praying mantis is the Bushman's god. They believe that Mantis is the spirit of their creation. The praying mantis sits in an attitude of great reverence, his head tipped to one side, as though he is listening — listening to the prayers of the Bushmen. There is an almost human look to a mantis face; it has a pointed chin, high cheek bones, and yellow skin. It is a little like a Bushman face. The big, bright eyes of Mantis seem to look right into the hearts of the Bushmen and to know their needs and hopes.

Makai began the familiar story. There in the cool morning, with a fire to warm them, the Bushmen gathered about the old man. The aroma of the cooking soup curled around them, and they were happy.

"One day Mantis came to a place where Ostrich had been eating his dinner. Mantis noticed a delicious smell

that he had never smelled before. He wondered what Ostrich had had for his meal. Secretly he followed Ostrich until one day he saw him preparing his lunch. He was cooking his food on a fire. Mantis had never seen a fire before, and the smell of the roasting meat was so good that Mantis wanted that fire more than he had ever wanted anything.

"When Ostrich was through with his lunch, he picked up all of the fire and very carefully tucked it up under

his wing. Then he walked away over the desert until he
met a friend, and they went on their way together.

"Mantis went home that day very thoughtfully. He
wanted some of that fire, but how was he going to get it?
He thought and he thought, and then all at once he had
a marvelous idea.

"He went very early the next morning to call upon
Ostrich.

"'Ostrich,' he said politely, 'I came to invite you to
go with me to the biggest yellow plum tree that you
have ever seen, and we will eat the plums together.'

"The Ostrich was delighted because he loved wild
yellow plums better than anything else.

"As they came to the tree, Mantis invited Ostrich to
eat first. Ostrich began at once to feast upon the deli-

cious fruit. And now Mantis said, 'Look, Ostrich, right at the top of the tree are the ripest plums of all. If you reach very high, you can get them.'

"Ostrich reached higher and higher, while Mantis urged him on. He stretched his wing to its very tip to get the most golden plum of all, right at the top of the tree. Then—just as Mantis had figured—the fire fell out from under Ostrich's wing. Quick as he could, Mantis grabbed some of the glowing coals and ran off with them.

"Mantis took the fire home and gave it to all the people. Then everyone could have roasted meat, and light in the darkness, and warmth in the chill of the morning.

"But Ostrich knew that he had been tricked. He had lost some of his precious fire. So he vowed that he would never again raise his wings; and to this day, he keeps them close to his side."

V

When the story ended, everyone sat quietly for a moment, thinking how clever and wise Mantis had been to get so good a thing as fire for the Bushmen. Then, since the soup was ready, breakfast began.

After everyone had eaten, the boys decided to play their stick-throwing game to keep warm until the sun got hot. One of the boys had lost his stick, and he had to make a new one. He selected a long slender branch from a special bush. With a bit of sharp stone, he scraped all the bark off of it until it was perfectly smooth.

27

Meanwhile the other boys had made a pile of sand. On top of this they arranged some smooth dry grass. The object of the game is to see who can skip his stick off the top of the mound and make it go the farthest.

The mound made, the boys all got in line, one behind the other. The game is played very fast. The boys began to run. Then at a certain place, the first boy threw his stick at the mound while he was running. After he had thrown his stick, he kept on running in order to be out of the way of the stick that was thrown by the boy behind him. Nuse threw his stick and ran to find where it had gone. Nxou was next.

Nxou threw with all his might, and his stick struck

the pile of grass just right. It went sailing off the other side of the pile and way off into the sand.

Each boy knew his own stick and when each had found his, they all saw that Nxou's had gone the farthest. So the next time Nxou was first in line. The boys ran and threw their sticks for hours, never seeming to tire of their game. They laughed and joked with each other all the while. And no one interferred, for the game was making their wind good, their legs strong, and their aim true. They would be good hunters when they were grown.

VI

While the boys played, the Bushmen women decided to build some new houses. When a house gets dirty or starts to blow away, the people just gather some tufts of the stiff, tall grass that grows in the desert and build themselves a new one. Everyone around helped, pulling up the bunches of grass and bringing them into camp.

A woman knows best how she likes her house, so the women did the building. They laid some branches together like an arch and then piled the grass around the branches and over them. The new scherm would be cool and shady inside in the daytime. At night it would give protection from the chill in the air after the sun had set. It took about a half hour to build a new house.

How wonderful it was to play, cool and secret, in a clean, new house. The pale yellow grass smelled of the sun and the wind; the red sand was soft and warm.

Gausje could sit there unseen by those outside in the hot, bright sunlight. What lovely dreams she could dream, hidden in such a quiet place.

It wasn't quiet for very long. Gausje's little sister surprised a lizard dozing in the sun-drenched grass and she chased it, squealing with joy. Gausje laughed when she saw them run by.

Then the little baby called Keikei ran up to Gausje and threw his short fat arms around her neck. Gausje loved to hold little Keikei. He was so soft and round.

After the chores were done, all the women went out into the desert to look for food. The men are the hunters of animals; the women find melons, roots and berries, lizards and turtles; and all the children go along.

Keikei was just learning to walk and his little legs got tired. Gausje picked him up and carried him on her back.

The women knew just where the plants that provide food for the Bushmen might be found. They wandered a long way over the desert, finding here a vine with a fat root below and there a melon or a bush with berries that would help feed the family. When a root or melon was still young and small, they left it to grow bigger. The desert is their garden, and they use it carefully. Everything they picked went into pouches, to be carried home. It was late afternoon before the search for food was over and the women and children started back to camp.

VII

Meanwhile some of the men were hunting. Others were just sitting talking or doing the things they liked to do.

Kamkope was an artist. He drew with pieces of charcoal on flat rocks. Sitting in the warm sun before his scherm, he drew things he knew. In the same way his ancestors drew and painted the things that they knew.

One ancient painting, in the land where the Bushmen used to live, tells a very strange and mysterious story. It is in a great cave and is hundreds and hundreds of years old. It was painted long before there is any record of white people being in Africa. In the picture there is a white lady, dressed in the costume of a Persian princess, with jewels and shoes. She is drawn in the way the ancient Egyptians drew people, with her head in profile and her shoulders facing forward. With her are hundreds and hundreds of dancing and marching black men. No one knows who she was or where she came from. She was there without a doubt. The Bushman artist who saw her painted what he knew.

In the same way, Kamkope painted of the hunts he had been on and the animals he had seen.

Andres, too, was drawing. He was decorating his ostrich egg. He had taken some charcoal and had ground it into dust between two rocks. Then he had taken some animal fat and worked this into the black dust. This made a black paste, something like oil paints. He put some of the paste on his toes, which he used as his easel. A sharp stick was his brush.

Makai was resting after telling his story. He was playing on his "gaeing bow" in front of his own scherm. Makai put one end of this musical instrument into his cheek, which he used as a sort of sounding box. He held the string taut and strummed on it with a short stick. The rhythm rose and fell and made a kind of tune.

We asked Makai how old he really was. He answered, "I am as young as the most beautiful wish in my heart and as old as all the unfulfilled longings of my life."

VIII

The men did not always sit as they did this day. One day when the family was all together, Aharob suddenly stood up. He had seen movement on the top of a sand dune. He shaded his eyes against the brilliant sun and looked again. There could be no doubt of what he saw. It was a gemsbok.

This beautiful antelope lives in the desert, although what it eats and drinks there during the long dry seasons is hard to discover. It is about four feet high, with spear-like horns four feet long. It's upper body is gray, and its underbody is almost white; a dark stripe on its flanks divides the two body colors. It has a black stripe down its back ending in a flowing black tail. The gemsbok is not a very fast animal, and a Bushman can run it down.

The Bushmen do not have meat to eat very often, and this day everyone was hungry. It was wonderful luck that a gemsbok should come by. Perhaps Mantis had sent it to them.

The Bushmen knew that they would be able to follow the tracks of the gemsbok and that they would be able to catch up with it. Quickly they got their arrows together and fixed the poison to put on them. The poison is made from the larvae of a certain beetle found at the root of a small bush. This poison will paralyze an animal's nervous system. It will kill a small animal within a few minutes, a larger one in several hours.

Andres carefully smeared some of the poison on the short stick that holds the arrowhead. Bushmen never put the poison on the sharp point because if they should accidentally scratch themselves, they too would die.

The shaft of the arrow is fitted loosely into the stick that holds the arrowhead. If the animal succeeds in brushing the shaft off in the underbrush, the arrow and its poison will remain in the animal. The poison does

not spoil the meat. Like most poisons used by primitive men in hunting, it is harmless when eaten. Only when it enters the blood stream through a wound is it fatal.

Nxou and Nuse were too young to go on the hunt. As the men got ready, the two boys took their bows and arrows and played that they were on a hunt, themselves. Bushmen believe that they can send out their wishes with an arrow. Nxou and Nuse shot their arrows into the blue sky and wished that they were men tracking a gemsbok.

The hunters were ready very quickly and ran off across the sand dunes in the direction that the gemsbok had gone. These men are able to run for hours and hours without seeming to tire and can often outrun an animal. They watched the footprints, which are known as the *Spoor*, of the animal; and they could tell by the way the grass was bent or a twig was broken just where it had been. It took several hours of running in the hot sun to catch up with the gemsbok.

When they sighted the animal, they fell to the ground and crawled along, keeping out of view and not making a sound. Soon they were close enough to shoot a poisoned arrow. The aim of the man who shot was true, and the stricken animal turned and ran. The Bushmen jumped to their feet and started in pursuit. They knew that very soon the poison would work and the gemsbok would drop to the ground. They tried to run it in a circle so that they would not end up too far from camp. When they were able to catch their quarry, they killed it quickly. Experts in all aspects of the hunt, they soon had the meat cut up so as to divide the load on their way home.

Bushmen never kill for the killing. They kill only when they are hungry. All of the animal is used. The skin makes a cover for a child, the bones make tools and arrowheads, and all of the meat is eaten.

IX

While the men were away, the women and children began preparations for the feast that would follow the hunters' return. With the same black paint that Andres had used to decorate his egg, the women decorated their faces. This was done very carefully, and the designs were changed for each person. The Bushmen have no mirrors, so each one had his painting done by someone else.

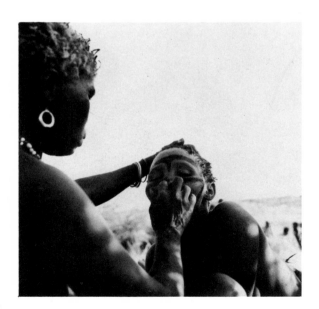

Nuse was pleased to have his face decorated. And like everyone else, he was excited. There was going to be roast meat for dinner; there had not been something that good for a long time.

Nxou alone was unhappy. His baby sister had fallen asleep in his lap, and he had to take care of her until

his mother was finished getting decorated for the cele- bration. His mother did not seem to understand that he had more important things to do. Nuse was waiting for him, and they were going to the desert to get wood. There would be a big fire that night, and they would need all of the wood they could find. The other boys had already started, and Nxou wanted to be with them. It was almost as good as going on the hunt.

By late afternoon the men were back with the meat. They had been very lucky. Sometimes it takes several days for them to track and kill an animal. This time they had done it in less than one day. The boys were back with their wood, too. Soon the fire was blazing. While the meat cooked, and a delicious smell crept over the camp, the dancing began. The Bushmen dance for everything: for birth and death, for happiness and sorrow. There is a dance to express every emotion.

This day they danced the Fire Dance. The women all gathered in a circle and clapped out the rhythm of the dance, singing together in a monotone, loud and soft, as the story unfolded.

The men danced in circle, around and around, pre- tending that they were the first Bushmen setting out in the darkness to find fire. The men looked and looked in the sand beneath their feet for the spoor of the fire, but nowhere could they find the footprints they sought.

They danced on and on, looking to the sun to help them, and then to the moon. They danced in the same circle until they had danced a deep groove in the sand. Still they had not found the fire.

Keikei watched the dance for a long time. Finally he got up on his little fat feet and tried to dance the Fire Dance himself. He pushed his feet through the warm sand and laughed because it was good to move through the sand and to dance with the men.

Keikei's little cousin watched, too. She couldn't get up by herself yet, so she could only look and wonder at what was going on.

Beyond the sand dune, a young springbok stopped to listen to the sounds. A pretty animal, with a pale brown back and a dark brown band on its sides, it might have interested the Bushmen as food at another time. But with a gemsbok on the fire, they went on with their dance and the springbok went on to join its herd.

Kamkope had been dancing for a long time in the hot sun, and he was thirsty. He took his ostrich egg out of his leather pouch and had a drink of the precious water.

The women clapped and sang on, and finally the hero of the dance found the fire and knelt down beside it, gathering hot coals in his hands and scattering them for all the world to share. The singing died away, and the men rested at last on the sand.

X

After the dancing, everyone feasted on the roast gemsbok. Then the children climbed the sand dune to play one of their favorite games. They rolled back down the hill and climbed up again. They rolled down backwards and forwards, sideways and upside down. It was wonderful fun. Nuse went down head over heels, all the way to the bottom.

Nxou ran all the way up one side and hurled himself in a great somersault over the top and down the other side. The other children all stopped to watch him. Then they went back to their own play. They got sand in their ears, sand in their eyes, sand in their curly hair; and they only laughed and rubbed it out again. There is little water in the desert, so Bushmen almost never wash.

Even little Keikei climbed to the top of the dune all by himself. He was very sleepy after the long day, but he wanted to stay up as long as the older boys stayed up. He was having so much trouble keeping his eyes open, that finally Nuse took him to bed. His mother scooped out a place in the warm sand for him, and soon he was sound asleep.

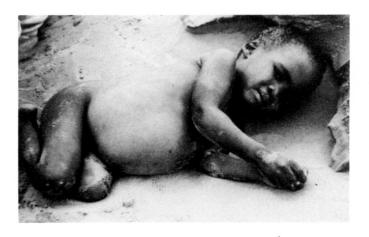

The other children were not long behind him. Each of them found his own hollowed-out place in the soft, warm sand and slipped off to sleep.

The night comes silently and swiftly in the desert. Soon the stars, seeming close enough to touch, began to twinkle down at us from the blue-black sky. The last bright rays of the sun caught for a moment on the tops of the great dunes, then faded from sight, and the shadows that had been lurking in the valley slipped quietly over them, hiding them from view. Sand does not hold the sun's heat as fields and forests, paved streets and steel buildings do. It was as though a giant heat lamp had been put out, and soon we felt the chill of the approaching night.

Now the mothers covered their sleeping children, carefully tucking soft animal skins about the little ones, who lay dreaming in their beds of sand, still warm beneath them.

More wood was placed upon the glowing fires. Laughter and conversation continued far into the night as the Bushmen gathered in small groups to smoke and eat. They were telling each other again and again the happy story of the successful hunt.

XI

As though it were yesterday, we remember this now: the still, starry night; the pungent scent of wood smoke; the musical sound of Bushman voices laughing and singing in the small bright circles of rosy light as they warmed themselves by their fires.

We remember the feeling of endless time as the silence of the desert night closed in.

Now, this night, many months later, as we sit by our own fire with the drifting snow about our house, we feel this again, remembering that somewhere far beyond our frosted windows, 11,000 miles away, our Bushmen friends are just waking up in their world of golden sand and azure sky. Nxou and Nuse will be running out into the desert in the warming brightness of the returning day. The long night is over, and another morning, fresh and new, lies ahead.

So it has been for 25,000 years—and so may it be until they wish it otherwise.

MARLIN PERKINS is director of the St. Louis Zoo, and CAROL MORSE PERKINS is his wife and is also the still photographer on the expeditions he makes to gather material for his television program "Wild Kingdom". Their trip to the Kalahari Desert to find and photograph Bushmen is not the only trip they have taken together. They have traveled almost everywhere in the world. Generally they are visiting not people but animals in areas where nature has been left relatively undisturbed by man. In more settled places, they tend to visit the local zoo.

Mr. Perkins is the author of *Zoo Parade* and of many scientific papers. He appeared on the television program "Zoo Parade" before the start of "Wild Kingdom".

Photographs Mr. and Mrs. Perkins took in the Lincoln Park Zoo in Chicago formed the basis for two other books, written by Elizabeth Laing Stewart, *Mogul Finds A Friend* and *The Lion Twins*.

AFRICA
LAMBERT AZIMUTHAL
EQUAL-AREA PROJECTION

SCALE OF MILES

0   200   400   600   800   1000   1200

SCALE OF KILOMETRES

0   400   800   1200

Capitals ....

International Boundaries ------

Canals ....

Copyright by C.S. HAMMOND & Co., N.Y.

CAPE VERDE ISLANDS
(ILHAS DO CABO VERDE)
(Portuguese)
SCALE OF MILES

0   50   100

Santo Antão
Porto Grande
São Vicente   São Nicolau   Sal
Boavista
São Tiago
Fogo   Praia

Long. West of Greenwich   20°   10°   0°   10°   20°   30°   40°   Long 50° East   of   60° Greenw.